101
Dog & Cat
Jokes for Kids

I.P. Grinning
&
I.P. Factly

Copyright © 2013 I.P. Factly

All rights reserved.

ISBN: 1494386178
ISBN-13: 9781494386177

DEDICATION

To Eleanor ☺.

1.
How do cats freshen their breath?

Mouse-wash!

2.
What dogs make the best hairdressers?

Shampoodles!

3.
What kind of dog goes tick, tick, woof, woof, tick, tick, woof, woof?

A watch dog!

4.

What kind of cat loves duck burgers?

A duck-filled patty puss!

5.

What animal has even more lives than a cat?

A toad - it is always croaking!

6.

What do nursing cats always carry?

First aid kit-tens!

7.

Why do you have to be careful when it starts raining cats and dogs?

You might step in a poodle!

8.

What do cats enjoy at breakfast?

Mice Krispies!

9.

Why don't cats and dogs dance together?

They both have two left feet!

10.

What warning sound do Australian dogs on bicycles make?

Dingo-ling!

11.

What happened to the man who crossed his dog with a tiger?

He had fewer friends visiting!

12.

What do you get if you cross a black dog and a white dog?

A greyhound!

13.

What is black and white and purple?

A Dalmatian holding its breath!

14.

What animal do cats like to sleep on?

A caterpillows!

15.

What happened to the little dog that met a lion?

He was terrier-fied!

16.

What did the dog say when it sat on some bark?

Ruff!

17.

Why do cats always have high scores on video games?

They have nine lives!

18.

Why are postal workers afraid of dogs called Frost?

Because Frost-bites!

19.

What dogs rip the mail every morning?

Tear-riers!

20.

What happened to the man who crossed his dog with an elephant?

I can't recall - but ask the elephant it'll remember!

21.

Why do dogs scratch themselves?

No-one else knows where the itch is!

22.

What kind of dog wears dark glasses and likes riding motorcycles?

A police dog!

23.

When would it be unlucky to see a black cat?

If you were a mouse!

24.

Boy: I lost my dog!

Father: Maybe you could put an ad in the paper?

Boy: That would be no good – he can't read!

25.

Girl: My cat swallowed a ball of wool!

Teacher: Oh no! What happened?

Girl: She had mittens!

26.

What are caterpillars' worst enemies?

Dog-erpillars!

27.

Why can't you train cats?

Because they think they are already purr-fect!

28.

Why don't you need a license for a cat?

You can't teach cats to lie down – you could never teach them to drive!

29.

What happened to the man who crossed a dog and a sheep?

He got a sheep that could herd itself!

30.

Why did the chihuahua bite the policeman's foot?

That was as far as it could reach!

31.

When should you take a pit bull terrier for a walk?

Whenever it wants!

32.

What was the greatest dog detective called?

Sherlock Bones!

33.

Why do dogs bury bones in the back yard?

Because they are not allowed to bury them in the kitchen!

34.

Why are big trees and little dogs similar?

They both have lots of bark!

35.

What kind of cat can perform somersaults and handstands?

An acro-cat!

36.
Where did the pit bull terrier sit at the movies?

Anywhere it wanted!

37.
What happened to the man that crossed a plane with a dog?

He found himself a jet setter!

38.
How do you know a dog eating fireflies is happy?

It barks with de-light!

39.

What do young dogs buy at a drive-in?

Pup-corn!

40.

What item from the bakery do young dogs love?

Pup-cakes!

41.

How do dogs stop the music?

They press the paws button!

42.

What did the dog say when it sat on a fallen tree?

Bark!

43.

How do you stop a dog digging?

Take away its shovel!

44.

Which dogs live in volcanoes?

Hot dogs!

45.

What is a young dog's favorite snack?

Pup-tarts!

46.

What is a young dog's favorite pizza topping?

Pup-peroni!

47.

What is a cat's favorite car?

Cat-illac!

48.

What cat purrs the most?

Purr-sian!

49.

What happened to the man who crossed a cat and a gorilla?

He got an animal that put him out at night!

50.

What kind of cats are disasters waiting to happen?

Cat-astrophes!

51.

What kind of cat loves mail order magazines?

A cat-alog!

52.

What happened to the man who crossed a dog with a lion?

He got an animal that barks at zebras!

53.

What kind of cat has eight legs and squirts ink?

An octo-puss!

54.

What happened to the man who crossed a cat with a lemon?

He ended up with a sourpuss!

55.

What kind of dancing do young dogs like best?

Body-pupping

56.

How do young dogs keep cool in the summer?

They lick ice pups!

57.

When does a cat go "woof"?

When learning a new language!

58.

How can you spell mousetrap with only three letters?

C-A-T!

59.

What happened to the man who crossed a cat with knee-length shoes?

He got puss in boots!

60.

What happened to the man who crossed a cat with the New York Times?

He got a mews-paper!

61.

How do you know your dog's been chasing ducks?

He's down in the mouth!

62.

How do you catch stray dogs?

Lie down and pretend you are a bone!

63.

What was the cat doing with cheese on its tongue and its mouth wide open?

Waiting with baited breath!

64.

What did the man say about the dog fed on rotten meat, garlic and old cheese?

Its bark is a lot worse than its bite!

65.

What do you call young dogs playing in melting snow?

Slush puppies!

66.

How did the dog untidy the house?

With a litter of puppies!

67.

What happened to the man who crossed a pit bull terrier and a seeing-eye dog?

It bit him then helped him across the road to the hospital!

68.

What do dogs do as a hobby?

Flea collecting!

69.

What do cats always watch at night?

The ten o'clock mews!

70.

What kind of dog always knows the time?

A watch dog!

71.
What do dumb dogs do?

Chase parked cars!

72.
What do dogs become after they are 12 years old?

13 years old!

73.
At what kind of market might a dog pick up something new?

A flea market!

74.

What happened when the man crossed his dog with a forest?

There was a lot of bark-ing!

75.

What did the dog get at dog school when it had to take six from nine?

Flea!

76.

What is the favorite color of a cat?

Purr-ple!

77.

What do alley cats like to do on a Friday night?

Go bowling!

78.

What happened to the man who crossed his dog with a cheetah?

It chased cars and caught them!

79.

What happened to the man who crossed his dog with a frog?

He got licked from across the room!

80.

What did the dog say to the cat prancing across its yard?

Nothing, dogs can't talk!

81.

Why does a dog get so hot at the beach?

It wears a coat and pants!

82.

How can you tell the difference between a suit and a dog?

A suit is jacket and pants but a dog just pants!

83.

What's even worse than raining cats and dogs?

Hailing taxis!

84.

How do dogs like their eggs?

Pooched!

85.

What did the cat get after visiting the doctor?

A purr-scription!

86.

What did the dog say at dog school when asked to take six from six?

Nothing!

87.

Where do you take a legless dog?

For a drag!

88.

What should you do when your dog chews a dictionary?

Take the words out of its mouth!

89.

What happened to the man who crossed roses and dogs?

He got a bumper crop of collie-flowers!

90.

Which US state has the most cats and dogs?

Pet-sylvania!

91.

What happened to the man who crossed his dog with a car?

He kept it in a barking lot!

92.

What is noisier than your neighbor's dog barking?

Four of your neighbor's dogs barking!

93.

What happened to the man who crossed a cat and a canary?

He got shredded tweet!

94.

What is the first thing a dog does when it jumps in a lake?

Gets wet!

95.

How much is cat food?

$2 purr can!

96.

Why do dogs always run in circles?

Because they don't know how many sides a rectangle has!

97.

What kind of dog should you use to find flowers in spring?

A bud-hound!

98.

What is a vampire's favorite dog?

A bloodhound!

99.

What goes Miaooooooooow?

A cat on a motorcycle!

100.

What happened to the man who crossed a dog with a killer whale?

He got an animal that barks at sharks!

101.

Why do dogs wag their tail?

No-one else will do it!

I.P. Grinning

ABOUT THE AUTHOR

IP Factly is the happy father of 7 and 9 year old boys. Their hilariously awful attempts to make up their own jokes inspired the IP Factly series of joke books for kids.

Hopefully you'll enjoy this book as much as he enjoyed writing it.

Made in the USA
Lexington, KY
20 April 2015